# VALUE CREATION
## — AND —
# PROSPERITY
## THRO' STOCK TRADING

**THOMAS ROMAULD**

INDIA • SINGAPORE • MALAYSIA

# **Notion Press**

Old No. 38, New No. 6
McNichols Road, Chetpet
Chennai - 600 031

First Published by Notion Press 2018
Copyright © Thomas Romauld 2018
All Rights Reserved.

ISBN 978-1-64249-520-1

This book has been published with all reasonable efforts taken to make the material error-free after the consent of the author. No part of this book shall be used, reproduced in any manner whatsoever without written permission from the author, except in the case of brief quotations embodied in critical articles and reviews.

The Author of this book is solely responsible and liable for its content including but not limited to the views, representations, descriptions, statements, information, opinions and references ["Content"]. The Content of this book shall not constitute or be construed or deemed to reflect the opinion or expression of the Publisher or Editor. Neither the Publisher nor Editor endorse or approve the Content of this book or guarantee the reliability, accuracy or completeness of the Content published herein and do not make any representations or warranties of any kind, express or implied, including but not limited to the implied warranties of merchantability, fitness for a particular purpose. The Publisher and Editor shall not be liable whatsoever for any errors, omissions, whether such errors or omissions result from negligence, accident, or any other cause or claims for loss or damages of any kind, including without limitation, indirect or consequential loss or damage arising out of use, inability to use, or about the reliability, accuracy or sufficiency of the information contained in this book.

## Dedication

I have my reverence to Almighty God and my thanks to my parents and family members especially to my son Stanislaus Ronny Terence who mooted the idea of writing a book on this subject, and for all the encouragements and their valuable support.

# CONTENTS

*Foreword* — vii
*Preface* — ix

1. Savings Are Not Equal for Investments — 1
2. Savings Are Essentially a Residual Process — 2
3. Wise Sayings from Financial Experts — 3
4. The Following Three Types of Assets Can Make One Rich — 6
5. Psycho Analysis of Trading in Stock Market — 8
6. Useful Terms to Be Known — 10
7. Revenue Growth — 22
8. Prices of Various Stocks – 10 Years Back — 24
9. List of High Divided Yielding Companies — 25
10. The Concept of Short Selling — 27
11. S.I.P – Systematic Investment Plan — 29
12. How to Watch and Analyse the Stock Index — 31
13. How to Place an Order for Buying the Shares — 33
14. Don't Prefer or Choose the Shares of the Following Categories. — 35
15. Companies Rewarding the Shareholders with Bonus Shares — 39

16. Documents and Details Needed to Open a Trading A/C with a Stock Broker — 42
17. How to Read the Accounts of the Company Statements — 43
18. Websites and Keywords for Reference — 47
19. Debt Burden — 49
20. Pre Open Session — 51
21. High and Low Ebbs of Share Prices — 52
22. How to Choose a Right Stock a Right Price — 53
23. Trading Process in Stock Market — 59
24. Top Five Sectors for Investing — 61
25. To Summarise — 63

*Epilogue* — 65

# FOREWORD

This book "Hand Book for value creation and prosperity thro' stock Trading" is not an end itself but a means to an end of valuable trading. This book lets the readers to have an access to stock trading and is very useful for students, learners, beginners in trading and as a useful tool, for reference.

It is a valuable reference for those, who aspire to make money for the purpose wealth creation in future. Trading represents short - term business, and investment is for long term. This book covers both these aspects.

I acknowledge and appreciate the valuable work done by THOMAS ROMAULD, with whom I am so familiar through his work and cooperation.

I wish him and the readers, the best of everything.

Dr. I. Francis Gnanasekar,
M.Com, MBA, B.Ed, Ph.D
Associate professor of Commerce
Vice-principal and HOD of Commerce Dept,
St. Joseph's College, Tiruchirappalli – Tamil Nadu.

# PREFACE

This book has been written mainly for those who are not familiar in the commercial world and are not well exposed to share trading but are interested in knowing and wishing to invest in stocks and shares.

This work has been taken up after very long thoughts, after seen that many popular books and magazines that do not teach or portray deep ideas and mode of investing in shares. On reading this book one will find the basic terms of the business as well as ideas for investing, when and where, in simple words and in easily comprehensible manner.

'Rome was not built in a day' likewise this work is after strenuous watching and monitoring of stock market, after a very long period, for nearly 30 years. Surely, these deep ideas will benefit the readers in a great way in wealth creation.

Thomas Romauld<br>Author.

# 1
# SAVINGS ARE NOT EQUAL FOR INVESTMENTS

Savings should be translated into investments. To save money one should make the withdrawals harder. Discipline of approach to savings is a must.

Savings are essentially a residual process, for a common man but for disciplined investor, savings first and use the residual income to spend, on current month consumption, (ie) by postponing current consumption to some extent.

Borrowing is, making use of future income, for present consumption, so borrowings should be avoided to the extent possible. One may borrow for unavoidable expenditure like Health, Education, Housing, etc. but do not borrow for buying luxuries. Do not borrow to help others, beyond your financial capacity. Don't borrow to buy happiness or pleasure; they will eat you up later. Don't borrow for the sake of investing, or buying shares and it is not a wise idea. Use your own earnings, for an unstressed growth.

Let your first expense, be your savings. Let it be your commitment.

# 2
# SAVINGS ARE ESSENTIALLY A RESIDUAL PROCESS

For an individual, any amount that remains after meeting current consumptions (expenses) is 'savings.' It would be instead a better one, if one saves first and then use the residual income to spend on current consumptions.

Savings should be made into a habit, to have a financially good future.

Every person in the world is looking for peace, within and around for which, one needs sufficient blood in one's own physic and sufficient affection at home with the family members and when goes out of his house, one needs sufficient money or else, one loses his peace within and also around. Therefore, for a holistic peace one needs good blood, good love and good money. Practically one can feel this. Therefore, this book tells the importance of investing habit. Remember Money is power and wealth is health.

# 3
# WISE SAYINGS FROM FINANCIAL EXPERTS

## What They Have Said

1. "To me money in abundance is paradise and power and love. In Scarcity, it is terror and guilt." – Bew Stein.

2. 'Don't let the mood swings of Mr. Market, Coax you into speculating and keep your emotions in check." – Warren Buffett.

3. Invest early, get your asset allocation right and above all, negotiate your salary. – Ramit Sethi.

4. Learn to be patient, and learn to be opportunistic. – Leon Black

5. My Best Investment Return ever came from picking a single stock. – Burtow Malkiel.

6. "Go against the enough, It takes hard work, a passion for what. You do and luck-Money enable you to put bread on the table at first, but it also enables you to give back in a big way. – Leon Cooperman.

7. 'Sometimes to make money, you have to spend it.' – Kelly Phillips Erb.

8. Save early and regularly and put most of your money, in a low – cost stock index fund – the magic of compounding returns – Jack Bogle.

9. 'Look at every single one of my expenditures and not to think about it, in today's dollars, but in future dollars" – Alexa von Tobel.

10. The key is to being rich is saving and saving early – Dan Ariely.

11. "If you are going to be passive, minority investor, don't do it with borrowed money" – Martin J.Whitman.

12. You need 10,000 hours, practicing to be good at anything – There are no short cuts – Row Baron.

13. Don't put your eggs in one basket' – Larry kotlikoff.

14. Keep one's spending in check – take concentered position – Bruce Green Wald.

    Finance is the technology, for making things happen.

    The poor works for money and the Rich makes money. Putting money away every month, is a sound idea.

    If you have any desire to be rich, you must focus on one idea.

    Focus and follow one course, until you succeed.

    Worst of times, is actually the best of times, to make money.

    Debt becomes a financial burden.

    The small cap stocks are used for fast growth.

    Money is power, respect it.

Academic intelligence and financial intelligence both are important.

Job – you work for others, to get money.

Investor – others work for you, to give you money.

Invest and be patient.

Don't worry when the market goes down.

Try to get financial independence.

Spend your wealth, to gain health.

Simplify your finances.

Priorities your spending.

Stream line your debts, debt means using future incomes, Avoid counting on tomorrow's income.

Pay your bills/dues in time.

Be realistic, in your expectations.

Keep your expenses low.

# 4

# THE FOLLOWING THREE TYPES OF ASSETS CAN MAKE ONE RICH

1. Real Estates – Land and Buildings.
2. Gold bullions (Not Jewells)
3. Stocks and shares.
4. Investment in Mutual Funds.

More money does not solve many problems but Intelligence solves problems.

He, who has the gold, makes the rules. Rich persons, Rich countries, Rich Communities, have rich gold.

Never forgo or sacrifice your health for the sake of wealth.

Early investing is a good policy. Earlier the better. I can quote many instances from investment point of view.

## For Instance

| No | Name of the scrip | Market price 10–15 years back | Current market price |
|----|-------------------|-------------------------------|----------------------|
| 1. | Honda siel | Rs. 7/- | 1348/- |
| 2. | Bosch | Rs. 1200/- | 23,000/- |
| 3. | MRF | 4500/- | 70,000/- |
| 4. | Mazda Indus. | 4/- | 332/- |

| No | Name of the scrip | Market price 10–15 years back | Current market price |
|----|-------------------|-------------------------------|----------------------|
| 5. | Honey well Automation | 1200/- | 12,000/- |
| 6. | Borosil glass works | 6/- | 6,271/- |

Those who had invested a few years back are being rewarded at present. Likewise, when you invest now, will reap a bumper harvest in later years, sow the seed now, in order to reap heavily and bundle them every seed takes time to grow. There is a germination period for every seed, as much as invested money to grow.

The Earthly system, we call it, nature, so to say, everything grows; both good as well as evil. If you borrow some money and if you do not repay it regularly it will grow up and stand like a big tree.

If you invest a small seed of money it grows and grows and ultimately into big tree, namely a Huge fund.

# 5
# PSYCHO ANALYSIS OF TRADING IN STOCK MARKET

1. In stock market, for instance, rapidly rising prices can cause more buys to enter, the market. At the same time, the entry of more buyers can cause stock prices to rise further away from their fundamentals. This is a good example of a positive steps to buy the shares at overvalued prices. It is called 'buying spree.'

   Likewise when the prices are falling everyone tries to sell the shares at the best possible prices because the same price, the same share may not fetch.

2. Therefore, the psychology of an investor is that when the markets turn down wards, many investors don't invest and refrain from doing so, even though, this is to best time to invest, for they are cautious about, further drop in prices, and wait. Likewise, when the market is very high, they don't invest, waiting for the market to dip.

3. **Be a Contrarian**

   If the market is extremely high, do not buy stocks in such environment, and do not sell you shares, when they are low. Do the opposite of what the market does, because, people tend to buy more, when the market is positive and going up and tend to sell at the possible rates, when market is down, or dull, thinking that, it will not improve, in near future.

Therefore, always try to buy at low ebb and sell at high ebb. 'This is called the 'contrary act' in trading.

Do not make the basic mistake of jumping into a stock, just because, 'its price is going up, up and up. Don't buy a stock, at high prices, just because, the price is rushing up. You have to invest only when the price comes down subsequently. The basic idea of trading is buy at low and sell at high.

Market is always operative in cycle. There are many forms of Business cycles, such as credit cycle, corporate life cycle, and market cycle. Business cycle, are like seasons of nature, will definitely happen and are inevitable, so the stock prices are not stable, rather reacting to the cycles. They go up and down, against our expectations. Therefore, a share price will have a high and low, every year. This is marked as 52 week High /52 week low as seen in the newspapers and magazines.

'The price that an investor pays for a share is not based on the fundamental value of under lying business, but on what other investor would pay for it.' will not yield good results.

# 6
# USEFUL TERMS TO BE KNOWN

1. Bullish market: It refers to when there are more buyers than sellers for shares.

2. Bearish market: It refers to when there are more sellers than buyers.

3. Lame duck: It refers to a person, who is unable to transact the shares of company, either buying or selling, on a particular day.

4. To book profits: It refers to sell the shares at the current market price, and liquidate the stock, even though, they are selling at a low price, due to certain circumstances.

5. Square off: To settle the stock a/c by selling the stock in hand, in order to make payment for the shares bought.

6. Carry forward: Any transaction is incomplete, say, no. of shares orders for either bought or sold, is carried over to next working day.

7. Margin: Any shares bought or sold, without having sufficient funds, either, it should be sold or bought before the end of the closing bell.

| | |
|---|---|
| 8. Delivery: | Means, ready to take up the shares, that have been ordered, on the same day of buying or the next day. |
| 9. T+1: | Means, Transaction Day (either buying or selling)+ one day. |
| 10. T+3: | Transaction Day + 3 days. |
| 11. Bought note: | It is the document, which shows the no. of shares bought, at what price, rate of commission and S.T. Tax etc. |
| 12. Sold note: | It shows the No. of shares, sold for the client with details. |
| 13. Buy order: | It is an order given by the client to the broken to buy no of shares of a company, at a particular Rate. |
| 14. Sell order: | It is an order/instruction given by the client to the broker, to sell the shares of a particular company at a specific price. |
| 15. Blue chip: | It refers to a valuable share, yielding good results, every year. |
| 16. Penny stock: | A very cheap share by price, available at a very low price, mostly around its face value. |
| 17. Statement of transactions: | It is a statement, sent by the broken periodically, to the client, showing the details of transaction carried out during a particular period, say. Monthly or quarterly. |

| | |
|---|---|
| | A statement of Transactions will show the names of the companies, number of shares bought/Sold, at what rates, S.T.T + brokerage, total transaction debits and credits, and the balance amount in the trading a/c, at the end of the period. |
| 18. Small cap: | A company, having less capital, which has less influence in the market, called capitalization. |
| 19. Large cap: | A company operating with huge capital, having much fluence in the market. |
| 20. E.P.S: | A company's net profit for a period, over number of shares issued, and what the company earns per share over a period. |
| 21. P/E: | It shows the ratio between current market price (C.M.P) the earning over a period. |
| 22. Opening price: | Yesterday's closing price, is used as a starting price for the next day morning on the start of the trading. (AT 9–15 in the morning) |
| 23. Closing price: | The price that is maintained at the time of closing the trading in the market – at the closing bell. (at 3.30 in the After Noon). |

| 24. Overvalued shares: | When the market price of a share is higher than the real value (ie) more than 20% of its E.P.S. (approximately) |
| --- | --- |
| 25. Undervalued: | When the C.M.P is less than or more less equal to its E.P.S it is said to be undervalued. |
| 26. Take over: | A company which is financially healthier than others, usually takes over other companies, which are either competitors or not well managed. |
| 27. Joint venture: | When Two companies come together, to do a business on contractual basis, for a specific period of time. |
| 28. Bonus candidate: | A well matured and financially established company is prepared to reward its shareholders with additional cash free shares, as Bonus. |
| 29. Cash cow: | A company having liquid-cash or easily convertible investment accumulated, from the past profit prepared to give high rate of dividends. |
| 30. Debt burden: | A company having borrowed heavy amounts from the public or from financial institutions, for its business, and unable to pay back, or struggles to repay both interest and principal amount as agreed upon. |

31. To Book-profits: Means to sell the particular shares at the present, in order to avoid future losses or further losses.

32. Pay out: Money withdrawn from your account held by you, with the stock broker.

33. Dividend payout: The total amount paid out by the company share holders as dividends, in a year.

34. Share broker or a stock broker: Refers to a person or a firm registered with the stock exchange (a licensed person) who is authorized either to buy or sell shares on behalf of its clients, registered with the firm.

35. Operating margin: This Ratio tells as how much, a company makes money from its normal business. It is derived by dividing the operating profit by total Revenues. A high operating margin is a good sign.

36. Portfolio: Refers to the list of investments, a person is holding at a particular period.

37. Bought price: After the shares are bought by your broker, he informs you the rate at which it was bought includes the actual price + S.T. Tax + his brokerage. Therefore it will always show a higher rate than the market price.

38. Sold price: This is the rate at which, your shares are sold. This will be less than the market price per share, as the S.T. Tax, and his commission has been deducted from the transaction.

39. Offer price: The broker when asked will tell you the rates different rates at which a particular share is offered in the market.

40. Bid price: This is the rate at which, you choose to buy the particular share.

41. Market ticker: A scrip code is called 'Ticker' In the place of the Name of the company, the code is used to avoid any doubt or misspellings.

42. Market driver: Particular trading day, certain shares show, the higher price, than the previous closing price and still go continue to grow, leading the Index, up and up.

43. Market draggers: There are certain shares, that pull the prices down, continuously, making the index on a day, to a decline trend.

44. Odd lot: When number shares, are bought or sold, in odd members like, 1, 3, 5, 7, 17, 21 etc instead of whole numbers like 5, 10, 100, 500, 1000 etc, they are called "odd lots." At present even one share of company can be bought and sold in the market after digitalization.

## Market Capitalization

It shows, how big a company is Market cap. is obtained by multiplying the stock price by its out standing member of shares.

$$\frac{C.M.P}{No.\ of\ shares\ issued} : M.cap.\ or\ Market\ cap.$$

A market cap of Rs. 5000 crs. is considered to be a small cap where as, Rs. 25,000 crs is a mid. cap. and the companies over Rs. 25,000/- are considered as large cap.

**Traded volumes:** Traded volume indicates how many shares of a company have been bought and how many have been sold, in a particular day. High volume shares means, that are easy to buy and sell at any date in the market. Called a 'liquid stock.'

If volumes traded are less means, very hard to sell and make money on that day and very hard to buy also.

**Dividend yield:** Dividends are the yearly profits, a company has made, that are shared among the share holders. It is arrived at by dividing the

$$\left\{ \frac{Dividend\ per\ share}{Current\ market\ Price} \right\}$$

The higher the dividend yield, the more money, one gets as dividends.

**Inflation:** It refers to increase in money circulation in the economy, which results in a fall in the value of the currency, thereby increase in cost of goods and services. Rise in prices is the result of inflation.

Inflation sinks your purchasing power, as today's money will not buy the same thing tomorrow. In order to protect against inflation, retirement planning should be done. Keeping the real, Rate of Return, in mind, which is the actual return from investment minus inflation Rate.

**P/E Ratio** of a company is calculated by dividing the current price of the share (C.M.P) with its earnings per share E.P.S (ie)

$$\frac{C.M.P}{E.P.S}$$ This P/E Ratio indicates

a number which is, unit of company earnings that an investor is willing to pay and hence it should be used to compare, it whether a stock is cheap or expensive, than the other stocks in the same industry.

Generally, P/E Ratio, is that the growing company would have a higher ratio as compared to low growth company and therefore P/E ratio is considered as a replacement to the growth rate of a company.

## Calendar Effect

One research work, shows the specific days for buying, Selling the shares in stock market, they are;

1. Normally share prices rule high on Wednesday – the best prices.

2. The month of December is the best time for buying and investing.

3. The shares price are high during the month of January, every year.

4. The volume of trade is on the high side during. I half of the year, rather than II Half of the same year.

5. The month of Oct, Nov, Dec, are the selling period of shares, and not for buying.

6. Trade is always in higher volume, before a public holiday or holidays.

## Securities Transaction Tax

This tax is levied by the stock exchanges on the shares we buy and sell, each time.

1. **S.T.T on Intra day Transaction** – 0.025% on Selling point (and not on buying)

   On Delivery basis – 0.1% on either side, both while on buying and on selling, on the volume of shares we buy and sell.

   **For Example**

   (Current market price x No. of share) X S.T.T. rate = amount of tax

2. **G.S.T** Goods and Services Tax is also payable while buying/selling @ 18% on the volume. (18% as for the year 2017, likely to be changed)

## Earning Per Share (E.P.S)

Any business is formed for the purpose of earning good profits, year after year. No company is established to make losses. The key purpose of business is to make profits. A company is valued by its earnings, through its sales. More sales, more income, more income, more profit. This should be understood before trading.

More profit, more returns to the share holder, called dividend. The Dividend is based on earning per share. Therefore, we are going to see something more on E.P.S.

This shows the profit earned by a company is an accounting year per share. A company capital is divided into number of shares. This capital is used to do business and earn profits every year. Hence, in order to measure the earning per share, the following can be used.

$$\frac{\text{Net profit earned in a year}}{\text{No of shares issued.}}$$

Say for example, a shares face value is Rs. 10/- and it earns Rs. 15/- in a year. This share is a good one to buy, because, of its value by earnings. If a person has bought a share in the market/or thro' I. P.O, at Rs. 10/- for some year back, he will be getting a profit per share of Rs. 15/- every year or more. If the EPS goes up then, earnings will be more. The company becomes very valuable in the market and the market price will also go up.

For example, the face value of the shares of T.C.S is only one rupee, whereas the current market price is Rs. 2246/-. (as on 15.07.2017), because it has earned and is earning a lot of profits every year. The E.P.S Rs. 135/- (2017) and 2750% Dividend at present. A company which earns several times of its face value is said to be a 'blue chip' company. That brings forth lot of profits to shareholders, clears its debt-obligations.

Normally, as seen in the past, Market price of a share will be 10 to 20 times of it E.P.S. If it is sold in the market, more than 20 times of its E.P.S, then the share value is considered as over-valued. That means you pay excessively, than its real value, to get the shares. The return of income will be less on holding it. As such they are not good for investing.

When, a company earns more, having more E.P.S, but the market price is very low, then it is considered as undervalued share. Therefore, the market price will go up in future and is worth buying.

What a company earns in a year in relation to its capital invested, is worth consideration.

### List of companies earning more profits per share currently

|    |                        | Face Value Rs. | E.P.S Rs. | C.M.P Rs. |
|----|------------------------|----------------|-----------|-----------|
| 1  | Ajanta pharma          | 2              | 54        | 1200      |
| 2  | Atul                   | 10             | 80        | 2194      |
| 3  | Bajaj Fin surv         | 2              | 149       | 5506      |
| 4  | Hero Moto corp         | 2              | 170       | 4047      |
| 5  | India bulls housing    | 2              | 72        | 1220      |
| 6  | Lakshmi Machine works  | 5              | 190       | 6124      |
| 7  | Maruthi Suzuki         | 5              | 245       | 7812      |
| 8  | MRF                    | 10             | 2515      | 65,145    |
| 9  | Reliance Industries    | 10             | 95        | 1609      |
| 10 | Schaeffler India       | 10             | 134       | 5027      |
| 11 | Shree Cement           | 10             | 365       | 17,779    |
| 12 | Vardaman Textiles      | 10             | 118       | 1217      |
| 13 | Wabco India            | 5              | 102       | 5484      |
| 14 | Page Industries        | 100            | 254       | 17898     |

|    |                  | Face Value | E.P.S | C.M.P |
|    |                  | Rs.        | Rs.   | Rs.   |
|----|------------------|------------|-------|-------|
| 15 | T.T.K. Prestige  | 10         | 126   | 6336  |
| 16 | Glaxo Smith CHL  | 10         | 149   | 5308  |
| 17 | Eicher Motors    | 10         | 643   | 31713 |
| 18 | Dr.Reddy's lab   | 5          | 72    | 2217  |
| 19 | Oracle Fin ser   | 5          | 146   | 3467  |
| 20 | Nesco            | 10         | 127   | 2439  |

# 7
# REVENUE GROWTH

Another important aspect one has to consider, before buying the shares is 'Revenue' growth of a company. Revenue refers to various sources of incomes for an organization. One must look into, whether the income increases or decreases every year after year. If the income increases, the can repay the debts if any, and become debt free in future. If the income decreases, the company cannot declare a good dividend and also the debts will increase and the company cannot become debt free. Watch out for the revenues, compare the revenues year to year; one will understand the growth of the company. For investment purpose a company should show a good growth in its revenues.

For instance: I. The revenue of P.C Jewellers, over the years.

| Revenue growth | | No. of show rooms | |
|---|---|---|---|
| 2012–13 – 4,018crs | ↑ | 30. | ↑ |
| 2013–14 – 5,326 crs | ↑ | 41. | ↑ |
| 2014–15 – 6,349crs | ↑ | 50. | ↑ |
| 2015–16 – 7,232 crs | ↑ | 60. | ↑ |
| 2016–17 – 8,099 crs | ↑ | 75. | ↑ |

**Instance: II: Bajaj Electrical**

| Year | Revenue Rs |
|---|---|
| 2009–10 | ⎫ Less than 1000 crs |
| 2010–11 | ⎭ |
| 2011–12 | 1000crs ↑ |
| 2012–13 | 2000crs ↑ |
| 2013–14 | 3000 crs ↑ |
| 2014–15 | 4,500 crs ↑ |

**III. Adami ports & SEZ.**

| Year | Revenue Rs. |
|---|---|
| Ending 2012. | Around 2,500 crs ↑ |
| Ending 2013 | 3,500 crs ↑ |
| Ending 2014 | 4,200 crs ↑ |
| Ending 2015 | 6,000 crs ↑ |
| Ending 2016 | 7,000 crs ↑ |
| Ending 2017 | 8,000 crs ↑ |

Likewise, a company's revenue growth, will lead it to the fore; as such one should definitely consider this aspect before investing, for further growth.

# 8
# PRICES OF VARIOUS STOCKS – 10 YEARS BACK

The value of the shares go up as years go by, so also their prices. The following shares for instance were selling at very low prices, some 10 or 12 years ago. At present they have become costlier because of two aspects viz. the growth of the companies by increasing their sales income and also due to inflation as a result of fall in the currency value.

| S.No | Name of the company | Market price 10/12 years ago | Present price (July 17) Rs. |
|---|---|---|---|
| 1 | Indra prasatha Gas | 16. | 1072. |
| 2 | Apollo Hospitals | 60. | 1274. |
| 3 | 3M India | 120. | 13236. |
| 4 | Bayors Corporation | 80. | 4,633. |
| 5 | Gillette | 240. | 5,110. |
| 6 | Nilkamal pastic | 30. | 1,884. |
| 7 | Page industries | 400. | 16,736. |
| 8 | Shree cements | 425. | 16,953. |
| 9 | Sundaram clayton | 60. | 4,398. |
| 10 | United spirit | 60. | 2398. |
| 11 | Hero Honda | 757. | 3844. |
| 12 | Honeywell Automation | 1331. | 12,673. |
| 13 | Gujarat Gas | 3. | 758 |
| 14 | Thirumalai Chemical | 16. | 1012. |
| 15 | H.D.F.C Bank (1995) | 40. | 1781. |

# 9
# LIST OF HIGH DIVIDED YIELDING COMPANIES

Investors can see the percentage of Dividend paid by these following companies, on their face values. As dividends are very high, their market price is also high and likely to go up further. They are worth investing. Before investing one should go through such lists for future gains.

| Sl.No | Name of the Co | Face Value Rs. | % of Dividend in a year | Market price (Aug 2017) Rs. |
|---|---|---|---|---|
| 1 | Maruthi Suzuki | 5 | 1500% | 7573/- |
| 2 | Bajaj Auto | 10. | 550% | 2754/- |
| 3 | Eicher Motors | 10. | 1000% | 30,648/- |
| 4 | Bosch | 10 | 1650% | 21,882/- |
| 5 | Sundaram Clayton | 5. | 630% | 4,489/- |
| 6 | H.D.F.C Bank | 2. | 550% | 1,772/- |
| 7 | Shree Cement | 10. | 1400% | 17,166/- |
| 8 | Gulf oil lubricant | 2 | 550% | 801/- |
| 9 | Peditite industries | 1 | 425% | 801/- |
| 10 | Tide water oil | 5. | 2,750% | 5751/- |
| 11 | HCL Tech. | 2. | 1200% | 880/- |
| 12 | TCS | 1. | 4,650% | 2489/- |
| 13 | L&T infotech | 1. | 1,655% | 740/- |
| 14 | Sona Software | 1. | 900% | 154/- |
| 15 | Jyothi Lab | 1. | 600% | 374/- |
| 16 | Hawkins cooker | 10. | 700% | 2705/- |

*Cont'...*

| Sl.No | Name of the Co | Face Value Rs. | % of Dividend in a year | Market price (Aug 2017) Rs. |
|---|---|---|---|---|
| 17 | Siemens | 2. | 1675% | 1255/- |
| 18 | L & T | 2. | 1050% | 1124/- |
| 19 | Cummins | 2. | 700% | 880/- |
| 20 | Coromandel International | 1 | 500% | 421/- |
| 21 | BSE | 2. | 1400% | 1004/- |
| 22 | Motilal oswal Fin. | 1. | 550% | 1329/- |
| 23 | H.D.F.C | 2. | 900% | 1765/- |
| 24 | India bulls housing | 2. | 1350% | 1221/- |
| 25 | Britania Industries | 2. | 1100% | 4247/- |
| 26 | Hindustal Zinc | 2. | 1740% | 286/- |
| 27 | NMDC | 1. | 515% | 123/- |
| 28 | Vedanta | 1. | 1945% | 299/- |
| 29 | Asian Paints | 1. | 1030% | 1141/- |
| 30 | Bajaj Corp | 1. | 1150% | 396/- |
| 31 | Godrej Consumer | 1. | 1500% | 804/- |
| 32 | Colgate palm | 1. | 1000% | 1087/- |
| 33 | Supreme Industries | 2. | 750% | 1124/- |
| 34 | Page Industries | 10. | 970% | 17203/- |
| 35 | M.R.F | 10. | 600% | 62805/- |
| 36 | TVS Sinchakra | 10. | 507% | 3350/- |
| 37 | CRISIL | 1. | 2700% | 1855/- |
| 38 | Hero Moto corp | 10. | 4250% | 3888/- |
| 39 | Amaraja Batteries | 1. | 425% | 767/- |
| 40 | Banco products | 2. | 450% | 205/- |

# 10
# THE CONCEPT OF SHORT SELLING

The principle behind the concept of short selling, is, where traders bet on share prices falling. This can be understood, at a simple example as shown below:

**A Stage I**: An investor or a trader approaches the investment fund manager, to lend shares or certain amount of money, to make a short sell. For example, 1000 shares are of a particular company is lent or its market value. So, 1000 shares of 100 each ie. Rs. 1,00,000/-

**Stage II:** In the hope of or expecting the share price to fall down, the trader borrows the shares, its value at its current price. (ie) 1000 x 100 = 1,00,000.

**Stage III:** The investor/ trader sells the shares at the highest price in the market. (ie) 1000 sh x 120. ie. 1,20,000/-.

**Stage IV:** On the same day, the investor/ a trader buys the shares of the same company, at a lower price, as the price has fallen down.

He buys 1000 shares @ 80/- per share. (ie) 80,000/- and give it to the fund manager. By doing so, he gains (120–80) 40 x 100: 40,000/-. Here, the trader, sells the shares at the first instance without having them, in hand, and then buy them and adjust it against the sale. This practice is called short-selling. This has been banned in several countries, but continuous in Indian stock markets.

Assumption are (i) the existing market price will definitely fall down the same day (ii) there should be buyers and seller for the same stock available. Sometimes, as against the wishes of the trader the price of the particular share, goes up; the concept of short selling, without having the shares in hand will not work out for wealth creation.

# 11
# S.I.P – SYSTEMATIC INVESTMENT PLAN

One need not be rich, to become richer, one's savings does not make a person rich, only the investment made out of savings makes, one rich.

Income – Expenses = Savings –> Investments. Mere deposits in the bank, cannot make one rich. They offer measly 4% p.a rate of interest on savings a/c and 7.5% p.a for one year deposits, but they lend at 14%–18%. Your money is safe, but does not grow to make you richer.

I can quote a very useful instance to show you the differences between savings and investments. A sum of Rs. 10,000/- invested in the shares of Wipro, in 1973, has grown and multiplied with Bonus and Dividends, over these years and has resulted into a total fund of Rs. 4/- crores, at the present value, of course over a period of 12 years. Can't one wait for such a short spell in one's life.

One need not invest, a bulk amount to get returns, whereas the investments can be made systematically (that means a fixed amount, that you can spare from your monthly income) say Rs. 1000/- per month and go on for 10 or 12 years, or 15 years, then you would see a huge fund, that you have created, beyond your expectations.

As such, you can invest your spare money, in good company shares, but not parking, then into a bank deposit, which also grows, but in a slow pace.

If your savings Rs. 12,000/- per year and for 10–12 years, it will grow and result in nearly 2.5 lakhs.

# 12
# HOW TO WATCH AND ANALYSE THE STOCK INDEX

Formally, there were 17 stock exchanges in India, in many state capitals, including Bombay stock exchange (B.S.E) later, National stock exchange (N.S.E) was created by the union government. So, at present there are only Two stock exchanges viz. B.S.E and N.S.E and are regulated by (SEBI) Securities Exchange Board of India. Both the BSE and NSE are situated in Mumbai. All the stock broker throughout in India, are well connected through internet, therefore on line trading is carried on during five days in a week (ie) Monday 'thro' Friday, having trading hours between 9.15 am to 3.30 pm. Saturdays and Sundays and Natural Holidays are holidays for stock exchanges. These stock exchanges, deal with, shares of companies, Debentures, government bonds and mutual Funds, called securities.

The name of the Stock Index of B.S.E, is called 'Sensex (Sensitive Index) of 30 shares. The name of the stock Index of NSE, is called 'NIFTY' (National Index of Fifty shares).

Even though there are four lakhs of companies, registered with the stock exchanges, the variation in prices on daily basis is considered on 30 companies shares in BSE and 50 companies shares in N.S.E.

The 30 shares of BSE and 50 shares of NSE are called Index Based stock or Indexed stocks.

**BSE:** On daily trading basis, the prices of 30 indexed shares are taken up and see whether the prices of which shares have gone up, in comparison with the opening prices and which ones have gone down.

If the price of a share has gone up, it is called 'Advance (Adv). If the price of share has gone down it is called 'decline.' Among the 30 companies shares (ie) indexed shares, more no of shares have advanced, then, it is shown as 'Index Advanced,' The symbol arrow is shown up wards like this (↑)

If more no of shares have declined than the number of advanced shares, then the index declined, show as (↓). At end of the trading session on a day, (ie) at the time of closing bell, it is decided whether today's market is or (Adv. ↑ or Decl. ↓)

Same is the case of NIFTY, taking advances and declines in the prices of FIFTY, Index shares. These advances and declines are result of very sensitive reaction of the share market, depending on the information received, in respect of performance of companies, results of accounting, issue of Bonus shares, right shares, taking up an order or a contract or a project. It may be as a result of national or international political changes, geographical impacts like, floods, rainfall, or drought, less harvest or even a disaster in the economy.

At present, the BSE/ Sensex stands at 3400.* Points level and Nifty at 10000 * points level. (* Index as on Dec. 2017)

# 13
# HOW TO PLACE AN ORDER FOR BUYING THE SHARES

Before placing an order, for buying a share/or shares, you should make yourself familiar and understand them clearly. They are, (a) Face value (b) current market price. (c) ordering quantity. They are explained below. **(a) Face value:** The capital of a company is divided into number of shares. First of all, capital is shared among many people. Secondly the profits earned by a company in a year, is shared among the shareholders (contributors to the capital Fund). At present, after many changes, the face of value of a share are in any denomination of,

Rs. 1/-, Rs. 2/- Rs. 5/- Rs. 10/- and Rs. 100/- Therefore before buying a share one should make sure the face value, for valuation and comparison.

**Example:**

| Sl.No | Name of the Company | Face value Rs. | Current Market Price (as on July 2017) |
|---|---|---|---|
| 1 | Asian paints | 1/- | 1125/- |
| 2 | Cipla | 2/- | 543/- |
| 3 | HDFC Bank | 2/- | 1683/- |

*Cont'...*

| Sl.No | Name of the Company | Face value | C.M.P (as on Aug 2017) |
|---|---|---|---|
| 4 | Infosys | 5/- | 977/- |
| 5 | Kotak Mah. Bank | 5/- | 962/- |
| 6 | Bata India | 5/- | 572/- |
| 7 | Eveready | 10 | 332/- |
| 8 | BEML | 10/- | 1717/- |
| 9 | BASF | 10/- | 1410/- |
| 10 | Ambika cotton | 10/- | 1320/- |
| 11 | Mon sonto | 10/- | 2484/- |
| 12 | Inter globe aviation | 10/- | 1313/- |
| 13 | 3M India | 100/- | 13,879/- |
| 14 | MRF | 100/- | 65,783/- |
| 15 | Bayer corp | 100/- | 4266 |
| 16 | Gillette | 100/- | 5354 |

# 14
# DON'T PREFER OR CHOOSE THE SHARES OF THE FOLLOWING CATEGORIES.

1. Companies producing products, based on Electronics (Not electricals) Such as mobile or T.V or any other gadgets, because, quite often, they are likely to be replaced, by an improved product or by some other Hi-tech companies, to make the existing product obsolete.

2. Products based on agriculture, other than milk products because of their seasonal nature (like edible, cooking oils), and failures in Monsoon and also earthly calamities, that affect the supply and profitability of the company.

3. Products based on Synthetics, that are unable to make the products stable, in the market and hence less profits for a particular period.

4. It is better not to choose steel companies at the present stage, as the production and distribution are regulated by the Government and also the input cost of raw materials, the prices of the final products are stressed by taxes and other import/export regulations that pressurize the iron and steel companies' profitability.

5. Don't prefer a company's share that does not have a wide market, ie, All India basis, known nation wide, and does not involve in any import on export because, it will affect the liquidity of the share. Sometimes unable to sell the shares in time and make money. You are made as a lame duck.

6. Companies producing sugar for consumption, as they are controlled and regulated by the local governments and center government pricing and pro current process based on government policies.

7. Don't choose, the companies, that involve in diamonds alone, as diamonds are not so familiar with the Indians, hence not much local sales.

8. Plantation companies, do not show, huge profits, or quantum jump in their incomes, as they are involved in agricultural process with high labour cost and other maintenance cost and regulations in labour, environmental issues, like fertilizers and pest controls.

9. Companies related to goods like textiles can be avoided (except a few).

10. Energy, power distribution companies suffer due to overrun cost situation, as such are unable to reward the shareholders.

11. Shipping companies are not earning huge profits, due to high labour cost, fuel cost, and other changes.

12. Try to avoid metal producing companies, as the regulations and input costs are stressing their profitability.

13. Avoid the shares of companies, having very huge debts. The debt equity ratio should be less than one. If a company has more debts than its Net worth cannot repay them and cannot give good returns to the shareholders. They cannot make you rich, if you have such shares.

## Rather, Prefer the Shares of the Companies of Following Categories

1. At present one can choose, the shares of finance companies, like Banking, NBFCS, esp. housing finance, business development finance etc. They are rewarding well.

2. Companies, producing medicines and bio chemicals, pharma, as they have a study and wide markets including worldwide exports.

3. Companies producing food items and eatables chocolates etc., as they have quick turnovers and also at a less cost.

4. Paint companies, can be preferred, as they are widely used in Realty sector, in urbanization process and Housing is a thrust sector, in India.

5. Companies, involved in petroleums, petro - gas and other petroleum based products, like lubricants etc. They are very profitable, due to constant demand for their products, in transport sector.

6. Always choose the companies, producing consumer goods (F.M.C.G) like cosmetics, Hair oil, toothpaste,

health drinks, footwear, garments etc. They are giving good returns to shareholders.

7. Regarding, companies like automobiles, airlines entertainments, I.T. companies, one must always be selective and choosy based on their E.P.S.

8. Companies producing milk products are very good for long term investments at present market condition.

# 15
# COMPANIES REWARDING THE SHAREHOLDERS WITH BONUS SHARES

A company can reward its shareholders in three ways viz.
1. By distributing dividends (of profits).
2. By rewarding with Bonus shares.
3. By giving preferences while issue of shares to the public, the existing shareholders have a pre-emptive rights over others.

Lets' talk about issue of Bonus shares to the existing shareholders. When a company is progressing, it would have made enormous profits through the years in the past. A company does not, distribute all the profits it earns in a year. A certain portion of profits is reserved for future developments or research and development, etc. These accumulated portion of profits are shown in the accounts as reserves and surplus in the balance sheet of a company on the liability side, because, these accumulate profits, over the years, belong to the shareholders and should not be diverted for other purposes. Therefore, the Board of Directions decide to issue, these accumulated profits in the shape of Bonus shares.

The existing shareholders, listed on a particular day called, 'The record date,' are only eligible to get the bonus share, at no extra cost, they are totally free. Bonus share always given in a particular Ratio (ie) Bonus shares for, every share held in the company. Say, 1:2 Ratio means a shareholder having 100 shares in hand will get 50 shares or 2:5, means, Two Bonus shares for every five shares held. Therefore a shareholder can multiply his holding at no extra cost. Bonus shares are not taxable, whereas, if the same company, has distributed the profits, then and there they would have been taxed under distribution Tax. Let me present a list of companies, issued Bonus shares in the recent past.

When a company has decided to issue Bonus shares in a year, it is called 'Bonus candidate.' The share price will automatically go up till the issue date, it is called 'Cum Bonus.' On the record date the Bonus shares are distributed to the shareholders, prices will tend to come down on the next day of the Record date.' Then it is called. 'Ex - Bonus price.' The list shows the Bonus shares issued by various companies.

## Examples

| Sl.No | Name of the Company | Ratio of Bonus | Record date |
|---|---|---|---|
| 1 | Petronet LNG | 1:1 | 9–5–2017 |
| 2 | Godrej Consumer | 1:1 | 9–5–2017 |
| 3 | ICICI Bank | 1:10 | 3–5–2017 |
| 4 | Bicon | 2:1 | 27.4.2017 |
| 5 | Wipro | 1:1 | 25.4.2017 |
| 6 | Muthoot cap | 1:10 | 18.4.2017 |

| Sl.No | Name of the Company | Ratio of Bonus | Record date |
|---|---|---|---|
| 7 | Ram Minerals | 4:1 | 14.2.2017 |
| 8 | Container corp | 1:4 | 13.2.2017 |
| 9 | V.Guard Industries | 2:5 | 30.01.2017 |
| 10 | Gail | 1:3 | 25.01.2017 |
| 11 | Advance Syntex | 3:20 | 15.11.2016 |

# 16
# DOCUMENTS AND DETAILS NEEDED TO OPEN A TRADING A/C WITH A STOCK BROKER

1. Name, as appearing in the Bank pass book.
2. Address proof, for correspondence.
3. Aadhar card details.
4. PAN card details.
5. Bank a/c No. and Bank branch, address IFSC No./MICR code No.
6. Mobile No.
7. Date of birth and occupation.
8. Cheque leaves.
9. Passport size photos.
10. Nationality – proof.
11. Status: Individual.

# 17
# HOW TO READ THE ACCOUNTS OF THE COMPANY STATEMENTS

Usefully as per Accounting standards followed in India, a company should publish in Newspapers or journals, their performance during a period say, Quarterly half yearly and Annual. At present, they are published in Newspapers Quarterly basis viz. Q1, Q2, Q3, Q4.

| Q1 | First quarter performance a financial year | From April to June |
|----|---------------------------------------------|---------------------|
| Q2 | Second quarter | From July to Sept |
| Q3 | Third quarter | From Oct to Dec |
| Q4 | Fourth and Annual | From Jan to March Next year |

As a financial or an accounting year starts from $1^{st}$ of April of a year through $31^{st}$ March of Next year (say 1-4-2017 through 31-3-2017).

| Starts | | | Ends |
|--------|----|----|------|
| Q1 | Q2 | Q3 | Q4 |

Now, we will see what the terms and expressions used in accounting. A company presents two types of Accounts viz. profit and loss a/c and balance sheet.

1. A profit and loss a/c shows, the quantum of the profit/loss, earned by a company, during a period.

[Total Income – Total Expenses = (+) profit /loss (-)].

2. A Balance sheet showing, the total liability of a company (liable to repay to the owners and creditors of a company). The total assets formed by a company in a certain period.

**Note:**

Any accounting figure or any amount shown/exhibited in Brackets are considered to be a loss or a minus figure.

For instance the E.P.S for this years (0.75) means the a/c shows a minus figure/loss earnings Nil, rather a loss, made by the company.

## The Aspects One Has to Look into While Reading the Accounts of a Company

1. Capital.
2. Debts of the company.
3. Reserves and surplus.
4. Net profit after Taxation.
5. Earnings per share.

Let's analyse and see their nature, how they affect the value of shares in the market **(1) Capital:** Some companies have a small amount of capital, say. Less than Rs. 100 crs, 200 crs. Some companies have large amount of capital, like Rs. 10,000 or 50,000 crs. The activities, of small companies the scale of operation or the projects undertaken cannot be a large one, They cannot extend their operations, beyond certain level. Therefore, their revenues from business activities, tend to be small or limited.

Hence they cannot bring forth, good EPS, say less than the face value of the per share. If you notice the market price of the shares, of those companies will be less and also won't go up much in near future. They need to expand their capital base or borrow from the public on interest. Therefore, it is better to avoid buying them for short-term & trading.

Certain companies with large amount of capital make business activities, can take up large scale operations. They have big business opportunities, like defence contracts, Railway contracts or any projects like construction of dams or even products required large numbers by the public. Therefore they can be bought for short term trade. Buying at low price, and see them, at a high price, because, their market prices always tend to go up early. The reason being, they bring forth large volume of profits and thereby high E.P.S.

There are certain companies, whose share prices in the market will be of medium rates. Say Rs. 150-/ to Rs. 500, can be bought for good investment for medium and long term. For instance, the share prices the companies like, M.R.F page Industries, Monsanto, Shree cement, Eicher motor, Britania, 3M India, were once, $1/20^{th}$ of the current market price. Once they were considered as mid cap but now they are very pricey.

For investment purpose, it is narrowed down, like this.

1. The shares of the large cap companies can be bought for short term purposes.
2. The shares of mid cap companies, for medium term investments like, three to five years period.

3. The shares of small cap companies, for long term investments, say to fifteen years period.

4. The companies which are unable earn E.P.S of less than their face values can be avoided.

5. Those companies, which are unable earn profits should be avoided.

# 18
# WEBSITES AND KEYWORDS FOR REFERENCE

Now-a-days, Stock trading is done via internet. The entire trading system through the country has been digitalized. If one goes into the website like MoneyControl where they provide visitors, the following details for reference before deciding on to buy a particular company's stock and this can be utilized for the purpose of trading. (there are other websites equally providing such information like economic times (ET), NDTV profit)

Details to look out for on these websites before buying or selling a stock:

Company News – Earnings, Stock-Advice, Management Interviews, Research Report, Sector- Board Meeting/AGM – EGM, Dividends, Bonus, Rights issue and Splits -Companies' Balance sheets, profit and loss accounts -Quarterly Results, Half yearly Results, Yearly Results, cash flow, Ratios, capital -Annual Reports: Directors Report, Chairman's speech. Auditor's Report-    Notes to accounts, Accounting policy. Finished products, Raw materials Investment structure. Share holding pattern, Mutual Fund holding, Top public shareholders, promoters holding Bulk Deals, Large deals. Peers- Similar Companies/Competitors-

Company Facts, Management, History, Background -listing and location. And mostly go for most recommended stocks

Some websites provide Mobile apps & Mobile Alerts too for those who are on the move.

## Suggestions

My best suggestions to the readers are, to read the financial Journals and Magazines regularly, and to keep oneself up-to-date, in financial information. The best way is to learn thro 'trial and error basis'. Practice makes one perfect. Therefore, try to buy and sell small quantity of shares, with low c.m.p, with low capital investment initially.

# 19
# DEBT BURDEN

Normally, companies used to borrow, loans from banks or issue debentures to borrow moneys from the public, but sometimes debts turn out to be a heavy burden on the companies, taking away cash profits and making dents in their E.P.S.

A company having borrowed heavy amounts for their regular business or for expansion, unable to pay back, both interest as well as repayment of principal amounts, as agreed upon. Then, what the company earns will be carried away by the lenders/creditors towards their interest amounts. Thereby less E.P.S. and less dividends and slow pace of growth of the company. Such companies find very hard to show growth in financial fronts. Hence, it is suggested that the shares of those heavily debt burdened companies may be avoided for trading, esp for investing.

Debt-Equity Ratio, is calculated as the Ratio between Total outstanding borrowings of the company, to its Total Equity capital, which speaks about how much a company, depends on borrowed moneys for its growth.

Usually, whether the D/E Ratio is less than two is considered to be a safe bet financially.

## List of Debt Free Companies

1. TATA Consultancy Services.
2. Cummins India
3. Zee Entertainment
4. Bajaj Holdings & Investments.
5. CRISIL
6. Infosys.
7. Bharat Electronics
8. I.T.C
9. Sun TV Network
10. Just Dial
11. Dr. Lalpathlabs
12. TATA ELXI
13. Persistent systems
14. ICRA
15. F.D.C
16. Ramco Systems
17. Alembic
18. KSB pumps
19. Quick heal Techno
20. Zydus wellness., etc.

# 20
# PRE OPEN SESSION

At present, the stock markets start trading at 9.15 in the morning with an opening bell. The prices of shares of different companies start increasing or declining depending on the mood of the market, but there are indications, and start placing order even before the trading starts. This is possible because of digitalization. The trend of the day follows the mood in the beginning. This is called pre open session. One has to watch the proper session, to follows the day's trade.

In case the prices fall or rise, it will continue till noon up to 12 o'clock and then starts rallying, continue the same position with minor changes in the prices.

**Closing bell:** The stock market closes at 3.30 p.m, as such the prices start reacting at 3 o'clock itself. If one wants to buy or sell any shares, it should be decided and done between 3 o'clock and 3.30 pm. Exactly at 3.30 pm it market will stop trading. The prices at that time are taken, as closing prices.

# 21
# HIGH AND LOW EBBS OF SHARE PRICES

High ebb and low ebb of share prices during previous 52 weeks period. Compare the prices and see the differences Buy at low and sell at High to make profits in Trading.

As on August 2017

| Sl.No | Name of the Company is short | High price Rs | Low price Rs. | Difference Rs. |
|---|---|---|---|---|
| 1 | Asian paints | 1230. | 850. | 380 |
| 2 | Bosch Ltd | 25,649. | 18,005 | 7,644 |
| 3 | Dr. Reddy's Lab | 3,394. | 1901. | 1493 |
| 4 | Hero Moto corp | 4019. | 2844. | 1175 |
| 5 | Indian bulls Housing | 1230. | 616. | 614 |
| 6 | Lupin | 1608. | 920. | 688 |
| 7 | Ambika cotton | 1430. | 765. | 665 |
| 8 | Avanti feeds | 1850. | 411. | 1439 |
| 9 | Bajaj Fin serv. | 5490. | 2515. | 2975 |
| 10 | BASF | 1809. | 988. | 821 |
| 11 | Bharat Bijili | 1498. | 719. | 779 |
| 12 | Dollar Industries | 2469. | 1314. | 1155 |
| 13 | Glaxo consumer | 6488. | 4650. | 1838 |
| 14 | Godrej consumers | 1083. | 642 | 441 |
| 15 | MRF | 74,100. | 35388 | 38,712 |

# 22
# HOW TO CHOOSE A RIGHT STOCK A RIGHT PRICE

First of all you have to check it out, whether you have sufficient amount in your running a/c with the broker or do have credits in your bank a/c to pay for that thro' a cheque. Therefore three aspects to be considered before buying a stock list of stocks.

1. The current market price of the share.
2. Multiplied by No. of stocks (i.e.) the quantity.
3. The total amount required for that transaction.

How to choose on identify a best stock for the value of money one is going to invest. Even again we go back to the E.P.S criterion. One has to check the current market price, (ie) the opening price on that day in the morning, even before the opening bell. So, one has to look into the previous day's closing price for the particular stock.

I can give you a practical example taking the actual price of a stock, viz. T.T.K. prestige ltd. The market price on the previous day i.e. on 11$^{th}$ Aug 2017 (FRIDAY) As the stock market, (NSE) is not functioning on Saturdays, and Sundays the previous close viz, Friday's closing price of Rs. 6246/- is taken as the opening price, on Monday morning.

Let's take up certain account figures looking out its valuation.

1. Current Market price – Rs. 6246
2. High and low in previous 52 weeks – Rs. 6824/4750.
3. The company's Equity capital – Rs. 11.666 crs

The face value of a share is Rs. 10/-

4. The E.P.S for 2016–17 – Rs. 129.38/-
5. Total Revenue on operation – 1,745.14 crs
6. The company's Revenues and surplus – Rs. 839.81 crs
7. The total capital employed by the co, is Rs. 11.66 crs, whereas it earns a Net profit of Rs. 138.59 crs, a year therefore, you can consider it as a good company and its Question is at what is the rate at which one should buy these share, at the current price or lower or higher.

General, rule in that buy at low and sell at high. Therefore we have to look into the previous 52 weeks high/low; it stands at Rs. 6824 high/ Rs. 4750, as it low price that has been sold.

| Low price | CMP | High price |
|---|---|---|
| Rs. 4,750/- ← | Rs. 6246 | → Rs6824/- |

The current market price stands at Rs. 6246/-. Therefore, one can take it for granted, the current price will more up to the previous year high point of Rs. 6824/-. There is a difference of Rs. 578/- one can get, on buying the stock.

There comes the valuation of shares. This company has earned a sum of Rs. 129.38 (say Rs. 130/-) as it earning per share. The value of a share goes by as per general rule, the market price of a share should be @ 10 times of its EPS on that year as its lowest price and can go up to 20 times of its

EPS. If we take this as into consideration the valuation goes as follows:

EPS Rs. 130 x 10 times = Rs.1300 = low price
130 x 20 times = Rs.2600 = high price

The share is valued as Rs. 1300/-as low price and Rs. 2600/- as its high price. But when you see the current market price which is Rs. 6246/-is over valued. The correct valuation can be around Rs. 3000/- If one buys this share, for more than the real actual value one pays excessively than its real worth. The return from this share will be very less.

Another example is as follows:

Thermax Ltd Face value = Rs. 2/-
C.M.P = 865/(as on Aug'17)
H/L of 52 weeks = 1070 /737
E.P.S = Rs.18/-
Therefore EPS x 10 times = 18 x 10 = Rs. 180/-
EPS x 20 times = 18 x 20 = 360/-

Overvalued shares should be avoided for investing and for returns. For Trading purposes the share can be bought, when comes near to its real valuation and can be sold when it goes up.

## The Price of a Share Is Likely to Go up in the Following Situations

If you are interested in stock market you should be in the habit of reading financial journals and magazines regularly.

There you will find the prices of various stocks going up. There are reasons for that. Let me list of out those fundamental reasons. for your future buying.

1. Where a company is about to announce, and distribute dividends to the shareholders, announced in its board meeting.

2. When a company is a bonus candidate, and about to announce bonus shares to the existing shareholders.

3. When a company, get a large export orders.

4. When the government gives tax relief, or concessions on a product or the the sector.

5. When a company goes for expansion of business, taking up new projects or introducing new products into market.

6. When a company earns bulk profits in a year.

7. When the head of a country comes to India, to win contracts from Indian companies, and also, our heads of state visiting abroad, to expand ties with other countries and win several contracts for our Indian products.

8. Where an Indian Company exhibits its products, abroad wins several orders for its products, that will fetch future returns for the company.

9. Where a company spends a lot of money, on advertisement, thro' campaigns or thro' various channels to reach the general public.

10. Where a company is merged with another company or taken over by a profitable bigger company, the share price of the former company, is likely to go up.

11. One Investment adviser, says "Money can be made, provided, one has done some basic research on the company, based on fundamentals or technicals and not just because, a stock is trading in two digits."

Therefore, one need not be too technical in stock trading but, should understand the system in which it works, by learning the fundamentals.

## The Share Prices Are Likely to Come down in the Following Instances

1. Where the government brings in restrictions or bans on certain goods.
2. When the rumour of war is around.
3. Heavy Taxation on certain goods.
4. When the profitability of a company comes down, with declining E.P.S Quarter to Quarter.
5. Where the competition is serve among the peer companies and other have certain competitive advantage.
6. Where there is a change in the board of directors in a company or a chairman/an M.D is changed.
7. Export Restriction introduced by the government.

8. Changes in the import policy of other countries for a particular product.

9. Where majority of the shares, held by the promoters, are pledged with the bank, for raising finance.

10. If a company or its Directors, involve themselves, in any scam or rigging in business.

# 23
# TRADING PROCESS IN STOCK MARKET

This chapter tells you how to buy and sell, stocks in an easy and phased manners. Therefore, do not rush to make an easy buck, but look for the one that is productive and long lasting.

Approach a share broker also called stock broker dealing in share trading, called Equity Market. Don't talk or have a conversation with a broker, over phone for the first time. Go directly into the office and contact them personally, with the person concerned on getting an appointment, regarding starting an account with the share broking firm for share trading.

Don't tell them what all you know, about share market, rather have your own ideas, ask them to explain, the trade and their views thereon.

Prepare the documents, both originals and copies, as they ask for, and fill up the forms, after due information from them. Sign them after, you have satisfied with their explanations. Don't rush, to do everything in a day.

Visit again, after few days, and talk to them that you have made up you mind, to get started, the actual trade. Choose a share broker, who is nearer to your residence or office whom you can approach, whenever you need, for clarifications, Don't choose the broker, who is far away from, your stay.

Even after you are familiar with the broker, contact them personally, periodically for information and for changes in regulations etc.

## Required Documents

1. Personal passport size photos.
2. Bank pass book.
3. Aadhaar Card
4. PAN card
5. Ration card or Residence proof.
6. Cheque book.
7. Mobile No. for contact.
8. Email id.

# 24
# TOP FIVE SECTORS FOR INVESTING

The companies in the business world are grouped/classified into different sectors. They come mostly under 15 sectors while investing in stocks. One has to look into the sector and choose the best valuable companies within the sector. All companies under a particular sector are not performing well and all are not yielding good results, benefitting the shareholders. Therefore, one has to be choosy among them. They are Automobile, Chemicals, Communication, Cons. Durables, Constructions, Diversified, Energy, Engineering, Financial, FMCG, Healthcare, Metals, Services, Technology and Textiles.

Among these sectors, the following are chosen the best for investing and trading, (order wise).

1. Financial
2. Automobile
3. Technology
4. Engineering
5. Health care
6. F.M.C.G
7. Chemicals

In these sectors select three or four, five companies to the maximum. Based on the data given earlier, and start investing little by little and accumulate the shares, year after year. Don't consider ups and downs in the market daily or frequently; look for long-term benefits. Don't buy penny stocks and accumulate them as returns can't be gauged by anyone, almost losses over a period.

Follow these ideas, given above I am sure, you will be a millionaire in your life time.

# 25
# TO SUMMARISE

**Step No. 1:** Choose any five best sector among the fifteen sectors.

**Step No. 2:** Choose the shares of one company from each sector.

**Step No. 3:** The best five companies should have an E.P.S of minimum ten times of its face value.

**Step No. 4:** Those best five companies whose current Market price should not be more than 20 times of its E.P.S.

**Step No. 5:** Those best five companies should not have any debt obligation.

Invest only in those five companies, throughout and do not deviate.

**Step No. 6:** Those five companies should be paying a minimum of 10% dividends to the shareholders for three years consecutively in the past.

**Step No. 7:** Start buying the shares of those five companies selected whenever you find surplus cash/Extra money in your bank a/c or buy those shares thro' S.I.Ps, every month, minimum of Rs. 2000/- onwards, even though less in quantity. Don't swim around the entire stock prices.

**Step No. 8:** Don't worry about the decline in the indices namely, Sensex or Nifty-Invest continuously.

**Step No. 9:** Refer to the topic No: 14, often.

**Step No. 10:** If the above steps are taken, you will definitely be a millionaire in 10 to 15 years' time.

# EPILOGUE

It is expected that every reader of this book, needs to read it again and again in order to understand the nature of transactions in the stock market.

This is not a text book, rather a suggestion manual, for those wish to enter and to trade in shares. Therefore, mere glance or wade through it, will not bring out good results. Refer to the guide manual then and there. The words used in this book are very few and less-hard to understand. As this book does not contain too many techniques or critical analysis, to baffle the reader, rather very simple and easy to follow.

Hope, it will bring forth good results and prosperity to the readers.

Happy and prosperous investing, for a better tomorrow.

www.ingramcontent.com/pod-product-compliance
Lightning Source LLC
Chambersburg PA
CBHW021017180526
45163CB00005B/2000